Certifiably Human

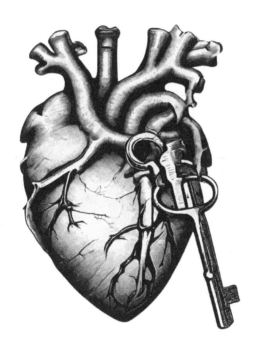

Beth Bottorff

This book is dedicated to anyone searching for their voice in this noisy world.

Acknowledgements:

I'd like to thank my circle of friends and family, those who have allowed me to be myself, no questions asked. Those who have inspired me to do more. To be more. Those who have mentored me. Those who have answered countless text messages in which I jump off the deep end of self-doubt and overthinking. Those who have held my hand physically and metaphorically during the good, the bad and the ugly times.
Without all of you, I wouldn't have made it this far.

A special thank you to:
Alexandra Parker, Jennifer Lock and Karen Ghant Hulvey for holding my hand through some of the structuring of this book.

Table of Contents

Chapter 1 ~ Just Me

The thing is,
She's a collage of pieces and parts
On a good day she holds her head high
Her shoulders free of worry
A passionate glint in her eyes
Creativity swirling pinwheels in her mind
On a bad day she bites her nails
Sinking under the weight of self-doubt
Overthinker extraordinaire
Her brain a rapid fire of
"What if, but maybe, I don't understand"
Mixed in with "when is it my turn"
She is at times an awkward attempt at friendship and
other times she's never met a stranger
On every day she holds tightly to faith
-At times as small as a mustard seed-
As she takes each day one at a time
The thing is,
She is certifiably human

Writing is an invisible girl's
Best friend
Ink and paper
Never straying far
Always lending a shoulder to cry on
An ear to rage to
A hidden safe for her memories and fears
A sanctuary for her hopes and dreams

Beneath the cardigan sweater
The clever tee and inked over flesh
Underneath the layers of skin
And bone
Under lock and key
There is a girl
Fierce and fragile
In her words

The thing is…
She's not put together and in control
Rather, she is frayed around the edges
Held together by a strand of hope
Vulnerability on the tip of her tongue

Stumbling over words
Tripping on shadows
Shy exterior
Held together with glue and daydreams

If you've come to find her
It's too late
She's gone
Living in clouds of music
Wrapped tight in fantasies
Taking a break from reality
You might try later
See if she's around

I dreamt I was
A dancer
Moving with grace
I dreamt I was
A lover
Adoring another
I dreamt I was
A musician
Giving the world rhythm
I dreamt I was
A writer
Delivering inspiration
I dreamt I was
A singer
Evoking tears
I woke up and found that
I was just me

Words cover her like a blanket
Memories like faded photographs
Eyes wide with hope
Heart wary

On some level, I think
She's always been lonely
And heart heavy

Maybe
Maybe she's just trying to figure out
Where she belongs

There is sadness in her eyes
And hope in her heart

The thing about her
The invisible girl
She takes the eggs from her basket
-sometimes-
Hurls them at the wall
So the disappointment
Is her own doing
And less like a knife in the gut

To keep it safe

-HOPE-

She hid it in a brick wall
Behind layers of brick and mortar
So deep no one could find it
And in time, neither could she

She takes a deep pull of alcohol
Unzips
Unbuttons
She steps out
Leaving a husk of skin behind
No longer needed
She walks with purpose
Toward the water
Slipping in
Over her head
Washing the dust
From her bones

Of all the scars on my body
Inside and out
Only the self-inflicted
Make sense to me
The reason for the pain
Blood
Scarring tissue
The reasoning crystal clear
Those make sense to me

Maybe you were conditioned
At an early age
To be afraid
To be invisible
To bail when life gets too hard
Maybe you brought all that baggage with you
On this life journey
Everywhere you go
Everyone you meet
Everything you do
Maybe you despise this part of you
It's okay to slough the skin
To change
To recreate
And break old habits
I think in fact
It's necessary

At some point in my adolescence
I crossed over to adulthood
Swept away in commonsensical
Dealings
But gazing at my profile in the
Mirror
I feel like an imposter
Just a child at heart

All her flaws
She wears on her sleeve
As if these badges
Dictate who she is

Self-deprecation
She has discovered,
Is a quick and easy way
To point out her flaws
In a badly drawn joke
Before anyone else can

Though she may fall face first
Stumble and trip
She bares her teeth
And
Plunges forward
All in

I wasn't wired to fight
I was wired to survive
Sometimes survival is hiding
Playing the peacemaker
Remaining invisible and silent

Invisibility served its purpose as a child
Ice queen in my twenties
Kept any hurt at bay
Now… Still as stone
Quiet so loud

She's rusty edges
Steely
Needles protruding
Caging in the vulnerability
She's a hopeless romantic
Dreamer of dreams
And if that were to get out
-the truth-
To escape the confines of her
Self-imposed reputation
Cynic
Muted
Emotions self-contained
The world would know her secret

It wasn't pride that kept her silent
It wasn't pride that held her back
It wasn't pride that encouraged her to bottle all the
emotions
-Vulnerability is a kind of nakedness-
It wasn't pride
She was wholly
Fully
Thoroughly
Terrified

Chapter 2 ~ Philosophy of a Girl

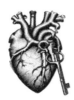

Q: How vulnerable do you want to be?
A: I want you to see my heart beating through a veil
of translucent skin and bones

Translucent
Adjective: semitransparent

I'll show you mine
If you show me yours
-scars-

In the end
What matters most?

You can't compare trees to dragonflies
It'll never work

Memories are funny things
At times a blurry flash
-Gone-
As if maybe they never happened

Fantasies are silly little things
Lifting you up up and away
As if riding in a hot air balloon
A height where every view is perfection
Eventually though
What goes up must come down

I think that sometimes
Desire can be
Fingernails on a chalkboard
Unslaked thirst on a hot day
Close but no close enough
No patience when patience is needed
I think sometimes
Desire can be
Agonizing
Excruciating

I've been told it's not safe to walk around my mind alone.
I might get lost.

Maybe on some level
We're all damaged goods

With each new sunrise
Comes a fresh new day
New beginnings
Raise your sword
Conquer

In her Desire to share beauty
She blossomed for all to see
A ravishing bloom
In his Greed, he plucked her
From the ground
Hiding her behind closed doors
To obsessively revel in her magnificence
And in her prison, she soon
Faded
Withered
Died

Chapter 3 ~ Alfresco

Staring up into the night sky
Begging the stars for answers
To the questions I harbor deep inside

Summer night
Sticky on my skin
Lightning bugs
Like flickering bulbs
There we sat all night
I wanted him to kiss me
In the end
He kissed her

You said nothing as we sat under the stars
Grass night-damp
You put your arm around me
Stuck your tongue in my mouth
I choked
Stuttered
Stumbled
You weren't the one I wanted to kiss

Golden rays of light
Slowly awaken and stretch
Reaching across the ever-moving water
While sanderlings race
Across the sand

I sigh with pleasure
As dawn spreads
A pink dust
Scattering across the brazen sky

Standing in solitude
At the waves' edge
Low tide
Coquina shells tickle my toes

Salty ocean brew
Foaming around my ankles
Invigorating

Riding the swell of the waves
A lone scrap of seaweed
Washes to shore

Saltwater waves
Lap at my feet
Washing away
Every day tension

The sun melts away
Leaving a pink night sky
I stand alone
Listening to
Whispers on the wind

Watercolor blue waves
Painted brilliantly with
Rainbow sherbert colored rays
Night is coming

Orb of night
Luminescent
I gaze up
Feel your pull

Chapter 4 ~ Memory Lane

How bad must it have been
That I can't remember?

Is it possible to recover from
An event or series of
When all you get are glimpses, whispers
Ghostly tendrils leaving trails of terror?

I never liked total darkness
My heart pounding louder than a jackhammer
And I can't catch my breath
Full on panic as
I fight to escape
What I can't see
Fear clawing at my throat
Silent scream
My mind reeling from a terror so real yet
My mind can't comprehend
Can't quite remember
I never did like total darkness

I asked God to show me
Help me to remember what really happened
So I could move on
A week of night terrors later and I think
The memories might kill me

How deeply do you want to delve
Into the recesses of memory
Long forgotten
To get an understanding
A sliver of light
Risking sanity
Inviting terrors
Soaked in tears
Choking on the dust and cobwebs
Is it worth it?

On any given day
She's covered in layers
Clothes that never fit
Drowning her body
Like armor to keep her hidden
Spikes and barbed wire
In hopes of protecting…
Invisibility being the goal, perhaps

Walking on glass
Feet bloody
Heart heavy
Reflexes at the ready

There she stood
In solitude
Staring into the void
Pondering the words
The words she had locked up inside her
Pondering the words
The words she ached to say
There she stood
In silence
Staring into the void
No words spoken
Trapped in the web of fear

Hey kid
Put on that thick skin
Shut it out
Pull it in
Close your eyes
Hey kid
Shut your mouth
You have nothing to say
And no one cares
They don't have time
Hey kid
Put on that thick skin
If you wanna cry
Bleed instead
If you can't breathe
It won't matter
Hey kid
Suck it up
Turn it down
Smash it to pieces of glass
That cut too deep
And bleed too red
And smear it
On your pristine paper
For only you to see
The pain you feel
That suffocates
Immobilizes
Sets that lump
In your throat
Hey kid
Put on that thick skin

One day I was your girl
Your sweet smiling girl
Next day I was a mistake
You said so yourself
In the kitchen
That dirty stinking kitchen
Where I held that knife
Sliced my skin
Watched the blood bead
And in that pain
I felt relief

The rusted edge of metal
Dragging across my skin
Felt better than the
Swirl of emotions that threatened to pull me under
#cutter

There in the water
Surrounded by darkness
She slumped her shoulders
Bowed her head
Opened the wounds
That refused to bleed out
Opened the wounds
That threatened to destroy
There in the water
Surrounded by darkness
She surrendered to the pain
Of too many yesterdays
Of too many broken
Too many broken
Too many broken
Of too much
Not enough
Bitter
Optimistic
Distrustful
Gullible
Too many
Tears
Too much
Blood
There in the water
Surrounded by darkness
In the safety of her lonesome
She surrendered
She let the tears fall

It's okay to cry now
Unabashedly
Unafraid
He can't hurt you anymore

I took it for granted
That little thing
Words bound
Covered in dust
Took up space I didn't have
I took it for granted
That I'd get around to it
Even if 3 times a charm didn't work
I took it for granted
That keepsake
Tossed out like trash
Because I needed to make room
I took it for granted
He's gone
It's gone
Neither one coming back

It was there in the dark
Deafening
Suffocating
That she realized
She wasn't ready
To let it go
To let it out
To share the pain
It was there in the dark
She realized
Admittance equaled reality
A reality she wasn't ready to face

Lost in old photographs
Rummaging around the memories
Of false innocence

I opened the lid
Unleashed memories
Words
Old pipes still smelling of tobacco
I read your words
Neatly typed on now faded pages
And for a minute, my heart broke for you

You know,
It wasn't **all** bad
It wasn't **all** good, either
At least we had Hemingway and Picasso

Chapter 5 ~ Too Much Noise

Too much noise in my head
At times I think I might drown
Choking on the scattered thoughts
Twisting in a deluge of
Incomplete ideas
That refuse to make sense
On paper

I can feel that downward pull
That hint of melancholy
Teasing around the edges
Blurred visions and comparisons
Teeter on the edge of my mind
Mixing with splashes of self-doubt
"Be gone!" I cry
"Be gone!"
I can't do this again

Stumbling
Falling
I'm sinking
On my knees and yet it still comes
This volatility
This shattered peace
That threatens to crush
To snap me like a twig

As I lie in bed
Sleep evades me
Yet again
My mind is a slideshow
Of what I am not
Of where I might go wrong
A slideshow of comparison
And what ifs
Drawing the blankets over my head
I frantically search
In the dark
For the OFF button

Some nights
-like tonight-
Sleep seems like a distant friend
Wanting so badly to reach out and grab hold
Some nights
-like tonight-
My brain is scattered in all directions
My thoughts scrambled
As if someone took a whisk to it
Some nights
-like tonight-
I'll stare at the ceiling
Willing my thoughts to calm
And my eyelids to grow heavy

"I'm just so fucking tired!"
Silent screams
Blurry tears
She straightens her collar
Smooths her hair
Dons her mask
Smile back in place

Maybe it's best
To play alone
Go on adventures alone
Dream alone
So as not to
Compromise what makes your heart shine

Chapter 6 ~ Trust

Hinges creak
Rusty
Ribs open wide
Cobwebs and dreams
Float on music laced currents
Vines entwined around
The innermost reaches
Thorns digging into
The edges of my heart
But…
But I think…
I think maybe…
You see me

No expectations
No demands
Just me
Just you

Maybe I had to drift
Through a sea of loneliness
To appreciate your friendship

Your charisma pulls me in
Like the always present waves
I'd freely ride your trough to your crest
And back again

Looking beyond your beautiful
Exterior
Peering into your eyes
The windows of your soul
I yearn to deep dive into your exquisite
Mind

Your vibe was such that
I didn't have to peel back the layers - one by one
As if stepping completely out of the skin was perfectly
Normal

I stand before you
Disrobing
Peeling back my layers of armor
Because I trust you
I lay bare my soul

Chapter 7 ~ Severed

You served me heartache
That late afternoon
As easily as if
Serving me tea

Through the misting rain
I saw his face in a fog
A vision of what used to be

Teardrops gather in puddles
As I watch your blurry body
Saunter away

It seems as if I've opened
Pandora's box
Stepping back into the past
Walking down memory lane
The good the bad the ugly
All on display
Broken hearts, undeniable shyness
Joy and hope. So much hope
Remembering the one man who ever made me feel
sexy and alive
And the absolute gut wrenching, can't eat for days pain
when he left
Reminded of the icy brick wall I became shortly after
Reminded of all the phases in my life
And I'm not sure if I'm better or worse for it.

With one hand you offer me light
The other, stone-cold darkness
What game you play
I've no idea
The rules are secret
Hidden in shadow
And I don't know how to play

Time heals all wounds
Yet time has passed
Moved on into another month
Looking down
I see only a gaping bleeding wound
Covered in humiliation
Seeping with disbelief
Oozing rivulets of red-hot anger
Time heals all wounds
Yet I still can't comprehend
What you did

He bit my ear lobes
One and then the other
Nuzzled my neck
Rough whiskered
Leaving a burn
Murmured lies
Shame on me
I should have known better

You've locked the door
Gasoline soaked
Flames alight
There's no way in
No way without the pain
That follows
She keeps trying
As if she hadn't already learned her lesson
As if she didn't already have scars

For too long
I believed
For too long
I swallowed your lies
Choking on the bitter wine
Your words driving me to my knees
Choking on tears
Apologizing for the curses **you** let loose
Self-worth
Self-respect
Lost
For too long
I believed
For too long

She almost drowned, you know…
Weighed down by the unrealistic
Expectations
Choking on the need to please
But then
But then
She opened her eyes
Pulled herself out
And walked away
She liked herself more than she
Liked him

I think I lost myself
For awhile
Looking into your eyes
Trying to be someone
I'm not

She stands on her hands
Feet touching the stars
Purging the sticky web of dreams
From her head

I dig out from the rubble of
Misguided intentions
False mandates
Lies of the world that take my
Breath
Leaving me gasping
Ideals that no longer suit me

Somehow, without realizing it
I gave you the key to my heart
I'd like it back

You opened the veil
Took my hand
I opened my ribs
One by one
Exposing my heart
I released the thorns
From which my soul was encased
Without a word or explanation
Gone like a ghost
And though you'll never know
How I truly feel
You may as well have shattered my heart
with your cruel absence

With a feral look in her eyes
Tears drawing lines in the dust
She wrenches her heart
From the cage of bones
She slashes
Cleaves
Rendering the organ useless
No longer a liability

She let herself mourn
Muffled sobs
Tears like ice
Burning her eyes
Tears like glass
Ripping her flesh
She let herself mourn
One day
One hour
One time
She shut the door
Tossed the key in the fire
And put on her mask of positive lies

My heart: she aches
Missing our connection
My brain: she reminds me of my tears
After you walked away without nary a word

I let you in beyond
My thorny gates
Gave you a piece of my soul
Believing you to be my friend
Yet you weren't, were you?
Your disappearing act would sting less
If I'd given you a piece of my body instead of my soul

Was it really that easy?
Leaving me in a web of confusion
Drowning in overwhelming silence
Flipping the switch
From friend to stranger
As if I were insignificant
Inconsequential and not worth your time

It'd be foolish
Dangerous even
To continue this effort of camaraderie
And connection
Knowing unquestionably
You can't give me what I need
And I'll end up drowning
In unattainable expectations

I almost hit send
This message to you
Sharing this song that
Causes all the feels
Remembering you severed that connection
I hit delete
Sending nothing
To no one

"You're a fool"
I whispered
A fool
Doing it all just the same as last time
Expecting a different outcome

I told myself I'd stop
I'd leave it
-you-
Alone
And here I am
Feeling like a clinging child
Grabbing pants legs
Exclaiming
"Hey!"
"Hey!"
"I'm right here!"
"Don't you see me?"

I thought I had a grip this time
Sturdy and long lasting
Yet
The fingers that dig into jagged rock
Slip
One by one
And yet again
I know how this ends
Plummeting
Deeper every time
Until the angry froth covers me
The raging water sweeps me away
Gasping and gagging
I go under

Chapter 8 ~ Faith

I am a vessel
Broken
Destroyed
Glued together again
Marbled skeins of golden light
Peeking through

My worth is anchored in Christ
I no longer chase after love
Disguised as crumbs
In lonely desperation

Despite my flaws
Ugly scars and vicious past
Steely fear
You came back for me
Held me as I cried
Your love is fierce

Me: Thank you for taking a chance on me.
God: You're not a chance. You're a sure thing.

What does it look like?
You standing near me
Hand on my shoulder
Holding me close
Despite the smears of dirt
My lapses in judgment
And continued offenses
The times I cursed and cried
Throwing myself into all
The wrong escapes
Yet you never left me
You held on to me
Pulled me in
Kept me close
Your love is greater than all of my stains

Despite the weight
Shoulders heavy with doubt
Shoulders heavy with longing
Shoulders heavy with fear
I stand tall
Knowing you are with me
Knowing you will carry my burdens
And walk beside me

I'm down on my knees
Head in my hands
Tears fall
Leaving dusty trails down my cheeks
Consumed in grief and fear
Believing lies that threaten
To tear me open
Lies that promise
Loneliness and isolation
Lies that promise the lack of purpose
Love and connection
I'm on my knees
Head in my hands
I hear a whisper
Small but mighty
I lift my face up
I hear it again
And though I cry
And though I'm on my knees
I hear it
"He is for you."

Chapter 9 ~ A Season

I can't help but wonder
Sometimes
When I'm alone in my thoughts
Is it too late?

At this point in my life
This chapter of loneliness
This chapter of yearning
For things so far out of my comfort zone
I can't help but wonder
If I've been forgotten
Left to fend for myself
Left to be a one-sided
Voiceless
Hollow
Shell

Sometimes I lay in bed
And as I wait for sleep to take me
I admit to myself
Silently
-to protect my secret-
That at times I am indeed
Lonely

Loneliness at times
Can sink its teeth
Deep into the heart
Tearing bleeding
Reminding me of what I don't have
Anymore
A light kiss
A sweaty passionate embrace
YET
YET
I'd rather feel the pain
I'd rather bleed out
Then sell my soul
Then sell my soul
For one night
Easily forgotten

It's going to be different
This time around
And going forward
No more crumbs
No more misaligned beliefs
That I only deserve
Sloppy seconds and trails of crumbs
I deserve the whole baguette
The whole shop

I'd rather be alone and wait to be someone's first choice
Then be lonely as someone's back up plan

I will no longer
Chase
Beg
Plead
For
Your attention
Your love
Your validation

Letter to Myself:

Dear sweet girl
Raise your head
You are not the past
Nor are you others' mistreatments
Take your eyes off the floor
Look ahead
Look up
You are worthy
Time
Effort
Love
You are worthy

It's okay
To feel loneliness
Maybe even disappointment
It's okay to want more
This isn't the end
This is just a season of healing
Recreating
Relearning
A season of lessons learned
This isn't forever

Loneliness can settle around
Your shoulders
Like a suffocating blanket
Snuffing out hope
Yet don't despair
It's not forever
It's okay
Allowed even
To do this life alone
If even for a season
It's okay
To refrain from chasing fumes of desperation
It's not a death sentence
You will survive

If I could go back and talk to my younger self
I'd tell her that no attention is better than negative attention
Curses and insults don't equate to "being seen"
Allowing someone to curse you into the dirt
While drowning in tears is never "good enough"
You are worth so much more than you realize
Do not let the past taint your self-worth. Do not settle for "good enough"
It's okay to stand alone until you find your people

Looking back, I don't regret much
Most people, events, and experiences
Served their purpose
And while it doesn't fit into
Lofty ambitions and high-status quota
I regret not dancing
In my twenties
At the shows every weekend
Caring so painfully what someone else might think
I regret letting the fear of others' opinions of me
Keep me glued to one spot
While my mind screamed at me
To go for it

A person's age, while just a number, can seem like
A sentence at times
A "time's almost up" reminder
A reminder of not being where you thought you'd be
Or doing what you thought you'd be doing
Even at times the lack of who you are with
And as such, a despair falls
Draped loosely around the shoulders
But what if
What if we could see age as an accomplishment
A goal post even
What if we were to see age as
"I survived 43 years. I'm still standing."

Maybe I'm afraid
Not of the what ifs
But of the hell yeahs

Maybe underneath it all
She doesn't want to be rescued
The knight standing tall
Ready to fix it all
Maybe she just wants to peel back her skin
Showing threads of vulnerability
Entwined in her bones
Maybe she wants to be told
"I see you."

Dismantle me
Tear apart the frame
Rebuild

What if this thing
This situation
This shit storm
That leaves me
Doubled over with pain and anger
Is really a chance
To start over?
From ashes come rebirth

While it might be a part of who I am
The past darkness
Baggage that threatens to make me buckle under the
weight
It's okay to let some of it go
Survival mode is no longer required

There will be days
Where everything seems to go wayward
Parking lot stumbles and lost glasses
Pushing hard
Reaching grasping for that goal and still
Still not quite there
There will be days that seem to drop you
To your knees
Screaming in frustration
On these days
-Because they will happen-
Go find the water
Watch the sun dance on her surface
Breathe
Linger for hours if need be
It is necessary

Did you really think you were special?
Did you really think you'd stand out?
It's that voice again
You know the one
The voice that - in the softest of tones -
Tears gaping wounds
Bleeding gashes
Threatening to destroy
Everything
The voice that in a moment of peaceful calm
Stirs up winds of doubt
The voice that promises to rip to shreds any semblance
of worth
Yet still, I get up off the ground
Straighten my shoulders
And move forward

Chapter 10 ~ Hope

You deserve someone
Who brings out the joy
Hope and magic in you
You deserve someone
Who you can freely be authentic around
You deserve someone
Who holds you in your tears
And in your ecstasy

When you connect with someone
Someone who understands
Your quirky weirdness
In all its glory
The fog of desolation
Forlorn as it sits heavy on your chest
Fades away

Covered in layers
Of dust and cobwebs
My heart is hidden
Deep deep within
Weighed down by rusted chains
Waiting for release
Waiting for you - whoever you might be

I want you to touch my body
The way you touch my soul

Brush the hair from my eyes
Trace my lips
Tenderly
Pull me close
So close I can feel your heartbeat
Against my breast
And whisper in my ear
"Your personality captivates me."

I'll trust you to sift
Through my garbage
And my gold

I would gladly
Walk across your thorns
Just for a glimpse
Of your rose

About the Author:

Beth Bottorff currently lives in South Carolina where the mosquitoes are the size of birds, and the legend of the Lizard Man lives on. She is the shy, nerdy girl next door who writes what she feels from day to day. Whether it's about a relaxing beach stroll or a traumatic life experience, writing has always felt like the one way she can express who she really is underneath. During the day Beth pretends to be an adult working a regular 9-5, although her creative, carefree spirit is never suppressed for long. She is a lover of nature, books, art, dogs, and all things silly.

Made in the USA
Middletown, DE
24 May 2024

54828021R00089